ALONE
WITH JESUS
Praying with the Gospels

Stephen Gabriel

Moorings Press

Falls Church, Virginia

Scripture quotations are from The Revised Standard Version of the Bible: Catholic Edition, copyright © 1965, 1966 the Division of Christian Education of the National Council of the Churches of Christ in the United States of America. Used by permission. All rights reserved.

Moorings Press
P.O. Box 6050
Falls Church, VA 22040

www.MooringsPress.com

Cover design: Kathryn Marcellino,
www.marcellinodesign.com

ISBN: 978-0-9827662-4-8

To the memory of

Jack Luther
1936 – 2017

A trusted friend and spiritual advisor

Contents

—⁓—

Introduction 8

Prioritizing Praying 10
    Priority of Prayer.................................... 10
    Prayer 12
    Power of Prayer...................................... 14
    Perseverance in Prayer 16

Living as Disciples 18
    Apostolate 18
    Sanctification of the World 20
    Divine Providence.................................. 22
    Narrow Gate 24
    Superficial Religion 26
    The Value of a Soul................................ 28
    Little Things 30
    Discipleship.. 32
    Denial of Christ...................................... 34
    Love and Obedience............................... 36
    Persecution 38
    Citizenship 40
    Instruments of God................................. 42

Pursuing the Virtues 44

    Purity 44

    Forgiveness 46

    Purity of Intention 48

    Detachment 50

    The Judgmental Soul 52

    Golden Rule 54

    Rock of Faith 56

    Faith 58

    Humility 60

    Corporal Works of Mercy 62

    Generosity 64

    Treasure That Lasts 66

Resisting Temptation and Sin 68

    Occasions of Sin 68

    Interior Sins 70

    Supernatural Outlook 72

Uniting to the Church 74

    The Pope 74

    Authority of the Church 76

    Rejection of Christ 78

    Light of Faith 80

    Christian Unity 82

Celebrating the Sacraments 84

    Marriage 84

    Mercy of God - Hope 86

    Born Again.. 88

    The Eucharist 90

    Confession... 92

Loving Jesus Christ.................................... 94

    Spiritual Childhood 94

    Generosity of God.................................. 96

    Spirit of Service 98

    The Need for Repentance..................... 100

    Christian Love...................................... 102

    Adoration of God 104

    Presence of Christ 106

    Importance of Good Example 108

    The Nativity 110

    Humanity of Christ............................... 112

    Obligations of Those Blessed by God.. 114

    Freedom 116

    Sanctifying Grace................................. 118

    The Way 120

    Our Dependency on Christ................... 122

    Friendship of Christ 124

    The Resurrection 126

Honoring Mary, Mother of God 128

    The Greatness of Mary 128

    Mary's Advice 130

    Mary, Our Mother 132

Accepting Suffering 134

    The Cross 134

    Mortification 136

    Christ's Passion and Death 138

Preparing to Meet God 140

    Ready for Death 140

    Promise of Salvation 142

    Heaven 144

    Accountability 146

    Hell 148

About the Author 150

Introduction

Many spiritual writers recommend using a book to assist us in our mental prayer. We can read a few lines and then bring them to our conversation with Our Lord. Indeed, many saints have urged us to take the Gospels to our prayer. Saint Ambrose said, "We have been given Sacred Scripture so that God and man may talk together; for we speak to Him when we pray; we hear Him when we read the divine saying."[1] More recently, Saint Josemaria Escriva counseled, "Do you want to learn from Christ and follow the example of his life? Open the Holy Gospels and listen to God dialoguing with men—with you."[2]

The considerations in this book were written to help me improve my prayer. I hope they can help you as well. Select a topic that you would like to consider with Our Lord, and prayerfully

---

[1] St. Ambrose, *On the Duties of Ministers* I, 20, 88: PL 16, 50.
[2] Escriva, St. Josemaria, *The Forge*, No. 322, Scepter Publishers.

read the related Gospel passages. Then you may wish to reflect on the considerations that follow. Some may resonate with you. Pay attention to those and take them to your conversation with Jesus. At times, you will not have specific words to express to Our Lord. This is a time for your heart to rest in him. It is enough to simply be with him, knowing that he is with you. You are keeping each other company. It is important to take the time to listen to what Our Lord is saying. He certainly speaks to us in the Gospels, but he also speaks to us in the silence of our souls. If we do not take the time to listen to him, we may miss the inspirations he is communicating to us. So, silently putting ourselves in God's presence and raising our hearts and minds to him can bear much enduring fruit.

May your Gospel reading, your time alone with Jesus, and your intimate conversation bring you closer to him and lead to a deep and abiding friendship.

Prioritizing Praying

—⁓—

PRIORITY OF PRAYER

Now as they went on their way, he entered a village; and a woman named Martha received him into her house. And she had a sister called Mary, who sat at the Lord's feet and listened to his teaching. But Martha was distracted with much serving; and she went to him and said, "Lord, do you not care that my sister has left me to serve alone? Tell her then to help me." But the Lord answered her, "Martha, Martha, you are anxious and troubled about many things; one thing is needful. Mary has chosen the good portion, which shall not be taken away from her." (Luke 10: 38-42)

Considerations

❖ My instinct is to sympathize with Martha. Mary's "idleness" offends my sense of fairness. But Jesus uses this situation to teach us an important lesson.

❖ Mary is at prayer listening to the words of Our Lord. He makes it clear that Mary's prayer takes priority over mere activity.

❖ My activity at work and around the house can be a prayer if I offer it to God and strive to do it very well.

❖ Jesus sought out Mary and Martha to spend time with them. He regularly seeks me out as well. How receptive am I to his overtures?

❖ Jesus, I need to spend more time alone conversing with you in mental prayer.

❖ Lord, help me to recognize when I do not give my time of prayer the priority it deserves.

❖ Forgive me for not making time for those daily conversations with you, Jesus.

PRAYER

"Pray then like this:

Our Father who art in heaven,
Hallowed be thy name.
Thy kingdom come,
Thy will be done,
    On earth as it is in heaven.
Give us this day our daily bread;
And forgive us our debts,
    As we also have forgiven our debtors;
And lead us not into temptation,
    But deliver us from evil." (Matthew 6: 9-13)

Considerations

- ❖ Jesus tells us how to pray very concisely in the Our Father. I will try to dwell on the different aspects of the guide he has given us.

- ❖ I adore you my God, and I praise you. Help me to seek unity with you now and forever.

- ❖ Lord, I want to do your will always. Please give me the grace to know your will for me.

- ❖ I am dependent on you for everything, my God. Move me to acknowledge this truth each and every day.

- ❖ Lord, give us leaders who will govern according to your will.

- ❖ My God, you have blessed me abundantly. I need your blessings now more than ever. I ask you to continue showering your grace and blessings on me and my family.

- ❖ Lord, you continue to forgive my sins and failings every time I seek your forgiveness in the Sacrament of Confession. I have let you down so many times, yet you never withdraw your friendship.

- ❖ Help me to imitate you by forgiving those who have offended me. Give me the grace to forgive even before I am asked for forgiveness.

- ❖ Lord, you know that I am weak and prone to sin. Assist me in avoiding those occasions of sin.

POWER OF PRAYER

"Ask, and it will be given you; seek, and you will find; knock, and it will be opened to you. For every one who asks receives, and he who seeks finds, and to him who knocks it will be opened. Or what man of you, if his son asks him for bread, will give him a stone? Or if he asks for a fish, will give him a serpent? If you then, who are evil, know how to give good gifts to your children, how much more will your Father who is in heaven give good things to those who ask him!" (Matthew 7: 7-11)

"Truly, I say to you, whoever says to this mountain, 'Be taken up and cast into the sea,' and does not doubt in his heart, but believes that what he says will come to pass, it will be done for him. Therefore I tell you, whatever you ask in prayer, believe that you receive it, and you will." (Mark 11: 23-24)

Considerations

❖ Prayer is truly powerful. Prayer can change hearts. Prayer can alter the course of human events.

❖ My lack of faith is the biggest obstacle to effective prayer.

❖ Jesus, I know that you want what is best for me. Help me to align my will with yours.

❖ Lord, you want me to ask for the things that I need, especially those things that I need for my salvation.

❖ Lord, may I grow in the virtues of faith and hope, placing my trust in you.

❖ Jesus, give me confidence in your Providence when my prayer is not answered in the way I would like.

PERSEVERANCE IN PRAYER

And he told them a parable, to the effect that
they ought always to pray and not lose heart.
He said, "In a certain city there was a judge
who neither feared God nor regarded man; and
there was a widow in that city who kept
coming to him and saying, 'Vindicate me
against my adversary.' For a while he refused;
but afterward he said to himself, 'Though
I neither fear God nor regard man, yet because
this widow bothers me, I will vindicate her, or
she will wear me out by her continual
coming.'" And the Lord said, "Hear what the
unrighteous judge says. And will not God
vindicate his elect, who cry to him day and
night? Will he delay long over them? I tell you,
he will vindicate them speedily. Nevertheless,
when the Son of man comes, will he find faith
on earth?" (Luke 18: 1-8)

Considerations

- ❖ Lord, give me the faith and the hope to trust in you. I know you will not abandon me.

- ❖ O God, let my prayer always be that thy will be done.

- ❖ Lord, teach me to conform my will to yours. I want what you want, the way you want it, when you want it.

- ❖ Lord, I know you want me to ask you for things, even though you know what I need better than I. Help me to accept your will and embrace it—even when it is not what I asked for.

- ❖ Lord, give me the grace of perseverance in prayer. I know you hear me. Help me to accept your timing. You know what is best!

- ❖ Dear Lord, help me to be convinced that when my prayer is not answered in the way I desire, it is only because you have something much better in mind.

- ❖ Lord, give me the faith to enable me to "pray and not lose heart."

Living as Disciples

—∿∿—

APOSTOLATE

And he said to them, "Follow me, and I will make you fishers of men." (Matthew 4: 19)

Then he said to his disciples, "The harvest is plentiful, but the laborers are few; pray therefore the Lord of the harvest to send out laborers into his harvest." (Matthew 9: 37-38)

"You are the salt of the earth; but if salt has lost its taste, how shall its saltness be restored? It is no longer good for anything except to be thrown out and trodden under foot by men.

You are the light of the world. A city set on a hill cannot be hid. Nor do men light a lamp and put it under a bushel, but on a stand, and it gives light to all in the house. Let your light so shine before men, that they may see your good works and give glory to your Father who is in heaven." (Matthew 5: 13-16)

Considerations

❖ What is Our Lord calling me to do? Does he want me to be a fisher of men, a laborer for his harvest, the salt of the earth, the light of the world?

❖ How can I fulfill this calling, given my current circumstances? What does it mean for me?

❖ How can I "let my light so shine before men?"

❖ Lord, help me to be the kind of Christian example I should be. Show me where I can improve.

❖ Lord, you are always putting people in my path. Show me what friends I can bring closer to you.

❖ Dear Lord, help me to expand my circle of friends. Show me how to be the apostle you need to re-evangelize my little corner of the world.

SANCTIFICATION OF THE WORLD

He told them another parable. "The kingdom of heaven is like leaven which a woman took and hid in three measures of meal, till it was all leavened." (Matthew 13: 33)

Considerations

❖ All Christians are called to be leaven in the world.

❖ Through my prayer and sacrifice, and Christian life and apostolic activities, I can make a difference in the world in which I live.

❖ I can influence the tone of society quietly through my dealings with my friends and neighbors, my coworkers, and my community.

❖ Jesus, help me to see myself as leaven in the world.

❖ Lord, show me how and where I can make a difference.

❖ Help me to get out of my comfort zone so that I can raise the spiritual temperature of the people with whom I associate.

DIVINE PROVIDENCE

"Therefore I tell you, do not be anxious about
your life, what you shall eat or what you shall
drink, nor about your body, what you shall put
on. Is not life more than food, and the body more
than clothing? Look at the birds of the air: they
neither sow nor reap nor gather into barns, and
yet your heavenly Father feeds them. Are you
not of more value than they? And which of you
by being anxious can add one cubit to his span
of life? And why are you anxious about
clothing? Consider the lilies of the field, how
they grow; they neither toil nor spin; yet I tell
you, even Solomon in all his glory was not
arrayed like one of these. But if God so clothes
the grass of the field, which today is alive and
tomorrow is thrown into the oven, will he not
much more clothe you, O men of little faith?
Therefore do not be anxious, saying, 'What shall
we eat?' or 'What shall we drink?' or 'What
shall we wear?' For the Gentiles seek all these
things; and your heavenly Father knows that you
need them all. But seek first his kingdom and his
righteousness, and all these things shall be yours
as well." (Matthew 6: 25-33)

Considerations

❖ I need to remember that I am always under the watchful eye of my guardian angel.

❖ Lord, I know you have a plan for me. Help me to entrust my life and all that happens to your Divine care.

❖ Lord, help me to remember Paul's admonition: "We know that in everything God works for good with those who love him…" (Romans 8: 28)

❖ When going through a difficult time, I try to remember that this life lasts for but a blink of an eye compared to my eternity with you, Lord.

❖ Things happen for a reason. O God, help me see the good that can come from hardships and difficulties.

❖ Lord, help me to realize that you are always present in my life. You are always close to me.

❖ Jesus, help me to grasp the truth of the fact that you would have suffered the agony of your Passion for me alone. You love me that much!

NARROW GATE

"Enter by the narrow gate; for the gate is wide and the way is easy, that leads to destruction, and those who enter by it are many. For the gate is narrow and the way is hard, that leads to life, and those who find it are few."
(Matthew 7: 13-14)

Considerations

❖ I know that I tend to take the easy way.
I seek comfort and ease whenever possible.

❖ That narrow gate includes small acts of
self-denial and acts of generosity.

❖ Specific and planned acts of self-denial can
help me to strengthen my will and respond
joyfully to Jesus' call for me to carry the
cross each day.

❖ Jesus, help me to have a plan of life that
brings me close to you—including prayer,
the sacraments, the Rosary, and Scripture
and spiritual reading.

❖ Lord, help me to develop a spirit of
sacrifice.

❖ My mortifications can have a redemptive
value, if I unite them to your cross, O Lord.

SUPERFICIAL RELIGION

"Not every one who says to me, 'Lord, Lord,' shall enter the kingdom of heaven, but he who does the will of my Father who is in heaven. On that day many will say to me, 'Lord, Lord, did we not prophesy in your name, and cast out demons in your name, and do many mighty works in your name?' And then will I declare to them, 'I never knew you; depart from me, you evildoers.'" (Matthew 7: 21-23)

"You hypocrites! Well did Isaiah prophesy of you, when he said: 'This people honors me with their lips, but their heart is far from me; in vain do they worship me, teaching as doctrines the precepts of men.'" (Matthew 15: 7-9)

Considerations

❖ Is the love of God truly in my heart, or do I just talk a good game? Actions speak louder than words.

❖ Do I take the Gospel message seriously and try to live my life accordingly?

❖ Jesus, show me where I merely honor you with my lips.

❖ Lord, you ask me to do the will of your Father. Please show me how to do that each day.

❖ You have told us to "love the Lord your God with all your heart, and with all your soul, and with all your mind, and with all your strength" (Mark 12:30). How can I begin to love you like that?

❖ Surely, doing the minimum in terms of prayer, sacrifice, and study will not bring me close to fulfilling this great commandment. Jesus, help me to love you with a generous heart.

❖ The thought of you telling me "I never knew you" is terrifying, indeed. I want a deep friendship with you, my Jesus. I long for your embrace!

THE VALUE OF A SOUL

"What man of you, having a hundred sheep, if he has lost one of them, does not leave the ninety-nine in the wilderness, and go after the one which is lost, until he finds it? And when he has found it, he lays it on his shoulders, rejoicing. And when he comes home, he calls together his friends and his neighbors, saying to them, 'Rejoice with me, for I have found my sheep which was lost.' Just so, I tell you, there will be more joy in heaven over one sinner who repents than over ninety-nine righteous persons who need no repentance."
(Luke 15: 4-7)

Considerations

- ❖ Everyone is capable of conversion.
- ❖ No one is beyond redemption. Atheists and hardened criminals can convert to lead lives of holiness. Indeed, that is just what Our Lord is calling them to do.
- ❖ At times, the realization of my sins and failures makes me feel utterly worthless. During these times, I have to remind myself that Jesus died for me. I am worth every drop of the blood shed by Our Savior.
- ❖ I have a responsibility as a parent to make every sacrifice necessary to ensure that my children receive the Christian formation they need to make the faith their own.
- ❖ Jesus, thank you for making it clear that one soul is worth more than any material thing. Indeed, it is priceless, of incalculable value!
- ❖ Recognition of this truth should influence my apostolic endeavors. Each person is worth my prayers and efforts to bring him or her closer to you, O God.

LITTLE THINGS

"He who is faithful in a very little is faithful also in much; and he who is dishonest in a very little is dishonest also in much." (Luke 16: 10)

Considerations

❖ Most of what we do are little things. If we do them with love, they become big things, important things.

❖ Little things accumulate into big things over time.

❖ If we wait to express our love in important matters, we will not have the capacity for love when the time comes.

❖ It means a lot to us when someone shows they care in small matters—a kind word, a smile, taking the time to listen, a small act of affection. It means a lot to Our Lord as well.

❖ An hour at Holy Mass, a few minutes of mental prayer, reading from Scripture and spiritual books, praying the Rosary—these are small things to offer my God and Creator, my Friend and Savior.

❖ There is no such thing as a "little sin." Although not all sins are mortal, they are all ugly in the eyes of God. Lord, give me a deep hatred of venial sins.

DISCIPLESHIP

"Truly, truly, I say to you, he who receives any one whom I send receives me; and he who receives me receives him who sent me."
(John 13: 20)

Considerations

❖ As a Christian, I am a follower of Jesus. I am his disciple.

❖ Do I really act like a follower of Christ— all of the time?

❖ I have been sent by God himself! This is a responsibility for which I will be held accountable.

❖ How seriously do I take my responsibility as a disciple of Christ? Have I prepared myself for this mission by studying the faith, frequenting the sacraments, and pursuing a life of holiness?

❖ Do I offer support to other disciples who may be struggling in one way or another? Do I initiate ways to collaborate with my fellow disciples in my parish and elsewhere to make our apostolate more effective?

❖ My discipleship is not a part-time endeavor. The need is so great! Lord, help me to see opportunities to proclaim the Gospel message to my family, friends, and colleagues in a natural and effective way.

DENIAL OF CHRIST

Simon Peter said to him, "Lord, where are you going?" Jesus answered, "Where I am going you cannot follow me now; but you shall follow afterward." Peter said to him, "Lord, why cannot I follow you now? I will lay down my life for you." Jesus answered, "Will you lay down your life for me? Truly, truly, I say to you, the cock will not crow, till you have denied me three times." (John 13: 36-38)

Considerations

❖ Peter loved Jesus deeply. Peter meant it when he said he would be willing to die for the Lord. But Peter was impetuous and weak—and Jesus knew that.

❖ I too have denied Jesus out of weakness. I have given in to temptation, despite my desire to remain faithful.

❖ Lord, do not allow me to despair as Judas did. Rather, move me to shed tears of sorrow and repentance as Peter did after his denials.

❖ Peter's love led him to begin again after his fall. I pray that I too can begin again—and again—after my denials.

❖ Peter professed his love for you three times after you had risen. Peter went on to shepherd your flock and ultimately give his life for you. Lord, help me to pick myself up after every fall with a sincere resolution to give my life for you.

❖ Peter became the rock upon which you built your Church. Lord, give me the grace to be the rock of faith among my family and friends.

LOVE AND OBEDIENCE

"I will not leave you desolate; I will come to you. Yet a little while, and the world will see me no more, but you will see me; because I live, you will live also. In that day you will know that I am in my Father, and you in me, and I in you. He who has my commandments and keeps them, he it is who loves me; and he who loves me will be loved by my Father, and I will love him and manifest myself to him." (John 14: 18-21)

Considerations

❖ Love! The world needs to know that the Catholic Church and its teaching are first and foremost about Love.

❖ Lord, I wish to love you the way you want to be loved.

❖ Worldly people will not praise a life of obedience. Help me to rise above worldly opinions and see that your commandments are the path that will lead me to you.

❖ I will strive to be faithful to your word, O Lord, in everything I do. The reward you offer is beyond my comprehension—the Blessed Trinity dwelling within me!

❖ The Trinity is a community of love. Lord, show me how to model the Trinity in my family and in other relationships.

❖ Lord, help me to see clearly that your commandments are for my good, for my happiness.

PERSECUTION

"If the world hates you, know that it has hated me before it hated you. If you were of the world, the world would love its own; but because you are not of the world, but I chose you out of the world, therefore the world hates you. Remember the word that I said to you, 'A servant is not greater than his master.' If they persecuted me, they will persecute you; if they kept my word, they will keep yours also."
(John 15: 18-20)

Considerations

❖ Lord, as I conform myself to you, let me welcome the persecutions that come my way.

❖ Jesus, you have promised me an eternity in Paradise. Persecution in this life is a small price to pay.

❖ O God, give me the fortitude to be faithful to you in the face of ridicule, attacks, and persecution.

❖ Strengthen my children, grandchildren, and all those who come after me. Keep them faithful to you and your Holy Catholic Church.

❖ Despite the persecution I may face, help me to always be cheerful and full of joy, knowing that you are with me always.

❖ Jesus, you loved those who persecuted you, forgiving them as you hung on the cross. Give me the grace to love the enemies of your Church—especially those who make my life difficult.

CITIZENSHIP

Jesus said to them, "Render to Caesar the things that are Caesar's, and to God the things that are God's." (Mark 12: 17)

Considerations

❖ Civil life is not conducted in a vacuum. All aspects of life should give glory to God.

❖ Do I have an understanding of the social teaching of the Church as it relates to such issues as the family, human rights, and work?

❖ Do I make an effort to know and understand the issues of the day so that I can vote responsibly?

❖ Any law that promotes or tolerates intrinsic evil must be overturned. What am I doing to ensure that civil laws are morally good and just?

❖ Am I completely honest when it comes to paying my taxes?

❖ Lord, help me to do my part in ensuring that civil laws are consistent with the natural moral law.

INSTRUMENTS OF GOD

But when Simon Peter saw it, he fell down at
Jesus' knees, saying, "Depart from me, for
I am a sinful man, O Lord." For he was
astonished, and all that were with him, at the
catch of fish which they had taken; and so also
were James and John, sons of Zeb'edee, who
were partners with Simon. And Jesus said to
Simon, "Do not be afraid; henceforth you will
be catching men." (Luke 5: 8-10)

Considerations

❖ To be an effective instrument, I have to be open to the promptings of the Holy Spirit. I have to be humble. I have to want to do the will of God.

❖ I need continual formation if I am to be an effective instrument of God in the world. I need to study Catholic doctrine, do spiritual reading, receive spiritual guidance, frequent the sacraments—and pray, pray, pray!

❖ Lord, you chose sinful and inadequate men to do your work here on earth. Do not let me use false humility as an excuse to say no to your call.

❖ It is you who does the work. You simply call me to be willing to be an effective instrument in your hands.

❖ Relying too much on myself invariably leads to disaster. Lord, help me to place my apostolate in your hands. When I rely on you, I am assured of success, even in the face of apparent failure.

❖ Lord, help me to unite my will to yours. Help me to want what you want.

Pursuing the Virtues

PURITY

"You have heard that it was said, 'You shall not commit adultery.' But I say to you that every one who looks at a woman lustfully has already committed adultery with her in his heart." (Matthew 5: 27-28)

Considerations

❖ Every person deserves to be treated with the dignity of one created in the image and likeness of God. Seeking to use another person is a gross misuse of my freedom.

❖ Do I guard my eyes when I come across images of men or women that are sexually provocative and may lead to impure thoughts?

❖ I go to Mary, my mother, whenever an impure thought enters my mind. She will protect me if I flee to her immediately.

❖ Pornography is a grave sin and can easily become an addiction that can ruin my marriage, my relationships, and my life.

❖ I want to have a zero-tolerance for pornography of any kind.

❖ Sex with my spouse is a gift of self. I strive to avoid merely using my spouse for my own sexual gratification.

❖ Lord, help me to have chaste relationships with those I date.

❖ O Lord, give me the grace to be diligent in avoiding problematic internet sites. I pray for the strength to consistently avoid these sites.

FORGIVENESS

Then Peter came up and said to him, "Lord, how often shall my brother sin against me, and I forgive him? As many as seven times?" Jesus said to him, "I do not say to you seven times, but seventy times seven." (Matthew 18: 21-22)

And Jesus said, "Father, forgive them; for they know not what they do." And they cast lots to divide his garments. (Luke 23: 34)

Considerations

❖ Jesus asked the Father to forgive his torturers while they continued to mock him, even as he gasped for breath while hanging on the cross.

❖ Is it pride that prevents me from forgiving?

❖ Jesus, you have forgiven me so much, and you continue to do so.

❖ Thank you for your forgiveness. Give me the grace to be truly contrite.

❖ Please Jesus, help me to change.

❖ Lord, give me a profound hatred of sin.

❖ Jesus, help me to remember those whom I have not forgiven from my heart. Am I waiting for them to express their sorrow and their repentance for having offended me?

❖ O God, give me a generous heart—a heart that forgives as you forgive.

PURITY OF INTENTION

"Beware of practicing your piety before men in order to be seen by them; for then you will have no reward from your Father who is in heaven." (Matthew 6: 1)

"And when you fast, do not look dismal, like the hypocrites, for they disfigure their faces that their fasting may be seen by men. Truly, I say to you, they have their reward. But when you fast, anoint your head and wash your face, that your fasting may not be seen by men but by your Father who is in secret; and your Father who sees in secret will reward you." (Matthew 6: 16-18)

Considerations

❖ May I give all the glory to God!

❖ How I love to receive recognition—and it pains me when I feel that I have been ignored or underappreciated.

❖ Do I take pride in seeing my name on the list of donors to charities?

❖ Lord, help me to be detached from the earthly rewards for my good deeds. Better that no one knows but you.

❖ When I find myself seeking the adulation of others, remind me, Lord, of all my defects and failures.

❖ All that I have—such as talents, gifts, position, and wealth—are gifts from God.

❖ Lord, you have blessed me abundantly. Help me to see myself for what I am—a mere tool in your hands.

DETACHMENT

"Do not lay up for yourselves treasures on earth, where moth and rust consume and where thieves break in and steal, but lay up for yourselves treasures in heaven, where neither moth nor rust consumes and where thieves do not break in and steal. For where your treasure is, there will your heart be also."
(Matthew 6: 19-21)

Considerations

❖ Lord, help me to regard my material possessions as gifts from you to be used for my sanctification and the sanctification of the world.

❖ Am I so attached to any of my possessions that I would be devastated if I were to lose them?

❖ Jesus, help me to be more generous with my money.

❖ Am I a "pack rat?" Do I have a hard time parting with things that I no longer need or use?

❖ Am I satisfied with the things that I have, or do I long for bigger and better things— house, car, neighborhood, electronic gadgets?

❖ Where is my heart? Is it fixed in this world, concerned primarily with material matters? Or do I have my eyes focused on eternity?

THE JUDGMENTAL SOUL

"Judge not, that you be not judged. For with the judgment you pronounce you will be judged, and the measure you give will be the measure you get. Why do you see the speck that is in your brother's eye, but do not notice the log that is in your own eye? Or how can you say to your brother, 'Let me take the speck out of your eye,' when there is the log in your own eye? You hypocrite, first take the log out of your own eye, and then you will see clearly to take the speck out of your brother's eye." (Matthew 7: 1-5)

"Let him who is without sin among you be the first to throw a stone at her." (John 8: 7)

Considerations

❖ Am I quick to judge others, pointing out their faults and weaknesses?

❖ I can judge actions as being good or bad. But I must not judge people. Only God can do that.

❖ I should be convinced that I am capable of the most heinous sin.

❖ If not for all of my blessings, I could easily be a most despicable person.

❖ Lord, help me to give people the benefit of the doubt. We are all "damaged goods" struggling in this life to do good, despite our fallen nature.

❖ I am a sinner, plain and simple. I sin in large things and in small. Lord, help me to examine myself deeply to identify my infidelities. Help me to make effective resolutions to overcome my weaknesses.

GOLDEN RULE

"So whatever you wish that men would do to you, do so to them; for this is the law and the prophets." (Matthew 7: 12)

Considerations

- ❖ How do I want to be treated by others? With respect, kindness, love, patience…

- ❖ When do I fail to live according to this "Golden Rule?"

- ❖ How do I act when I drive the car? Am I impatient, rude, pushy?

- ❖ Am I quick to apologize when I fail to treat someone the way I should?

- ❖ As a Christian, could my coarse behavior drive a wedge between the people with whom I deal and Jesus Christ? This kind of behavior is inconsistent with the life of an apostle.

- ❖ Lord, show me the individuals whom I treat with less respect and patience than I should.

- ❖ My God, give me the grace to see my failures in this area and help me to change.

ROCK OF FAITH

"Every one then who hears these words of mine and does them will be like a wise man who built his house upon the rock; and the rain fell, and the floods came, and the winds blew and beat upon that house, but it did not fall, because it had been founded on the rock. And every one who hears these words of mine and does not do them will be like a foolish man who built his house upon the sand; and the rain fell, and the floods came, and the winds blew and beat against that house, and it fell; and great was the fall of it." (Matthew 7: 24-27)

Considerations

❖ I can bolster my faith through prayer and study. If I ignore these means to grow spiritually, I have only myself to blame if I perish in the storm.

❖ Relying on myself, my own strength, my intelligence, and my talents amounts to building my house on sand. How foolish indeed!

❖ Lord, increase my faith!

❖ Jesus, I can get through any storm with you by my side.

❖ When I feel weakest and unable to persevere, I look to you, Lord, for strength.

❖ Jesus, you are my Rock, my Friend, my God.

FAITH

As he entered Caper'na-um, a centurion came
forward to him, beseeching him and saying,
"Lord, my servant is lying paralyzed at home,
in terrible distress." And he said to him, "I will
come and heal him." But the centurion
answered him, "Lord, I am not worthy to have
you come under my roof; but only say the
word, and my servant will be healed. For I am
a man under authority, with soldiers under me;
and I say to one, 'Go,' and he goes, and to
another, 'Come,' and he comes, and to my
slave, 'Do this,' and he does it." When Jesus
heard him, he marveled, and said to those who
followed him, "Truly, I say to you, not even in
Israel have I found such faith."
(Matthew 8: 5-10)

Considerations

- ❖ Faith is a gift from almighty God. It was infused into my soul at my baptism, along with the virtues of hope and love.

- ❖ Although faith is not the most important virtue, it is crucial for my salvation.

- ❖ With the faith of a mustard seed, I will move mountains in my apostolic endeavors.

- ❖ Lord, throughout your public life you were moved by the faith of those who sought your help. It seemed that you could not resist them.

- ❖ Help me to pray with the faith of the Roman centurion.

- ❖ Jesus, I pray that my love for you will enkindle a desire in me for an abiding faith.

- ❖ Lord, I know that my faith is not as strong as it should be. It can be shaky at times. Please, you know that "I believe; help my unbelief!" (Mark 9: 24).

HUMILITY

"Two men went up into the temple to pray, one
a Pharisee and the other a tax collector. The
Pharisee stood and prayed thus with himself,
'God, I thank thee that I am not like other men,
extortioners, unjust, adulterers, or even like
this tax collector. I fast twice a week, I give
tithes of all that I get.' But the tax collector,
standing far off, would not even lift up his eyes
to heaven, but beat his breast, saying, 'God, be
merciful to me a sinner!' I tell you, this man
went down to his house justified rather than the
other; for every one who exalts himself will be
humbled, but he who humbles himself will be
exalted." (Luke 18: 10-14)

"He must increase, but I must decrease."
(John 3: 30)

Considerations

❖ Humility tells me that everything I have has been given to me. Everything is a gift from my Father, God.

❖ My pride is the greatest obstacle to growing in the interior life. Indeed, it is likely to be the greatest impediment to my salvation.

❖ Pride rears its ugly head in so many ways— when I am corrected, when I revel in my successes, when I compare my family to others, even when I consider that I am a faithful Catholic and others are not. The list goes on.

❖ If I am not "like other men," it is only due to the grace of God. The truth is that I actually am "like other men!"

❖ Lord, fill my heart with gratitude for the gifts you have given me. I shudder to think where I would be without your grace and support.

❖ Lord, help me to be more child-like and more trusting in my relationship with you. I am utterly reliant on you, dear God. I need your grace, your guidance, and inspiration.

❖ My God, you must increase, and I must decrease.

CORPORAL WORKS OF MERCY

"When the Son of man comes in his glory, and
all the angels with him, then he will sit on his
glorious throne. Before him will be gathered
all the nations, and he will separate them one
from another as a shepherd separates the sheep
from the goats, and he will place the sheep at
his right hand, but the goats at the left. Then
the King will say to those at his right hand,
'Come, O blessed of my Father, inherit the
kingdom prepared for you from the foundation
of the world; for I was hungry and you gave
me food … 'Truly, I say to you, as you did it to
one of the least of these my brethren, you did it
to me.'" (Matthew 25: 31-40)

Considerations

❖ I focus too often on my needs and concerns and ignore the needs of others.

❖ Lord, help me to see your face in the faces of the poor and needy.

❖ How can I do more to serve you among the least of your brethren?

❖ It is good for me to give money to organizations that serve the poor. But, how about my time? Lord, show me how I can give more of myself in the service of your little ones.

❖ Jesus, show me how to love all those around me.

❖ It is my love for you, Lord, that moves me to care for those in need.

GENEROSITY

And he sat down opposite the treasury, and
watched the multitude putting money into the
treasury. Many rich people put in large sums.
And a poor widow came, and put in two
copper coins, which make a penny. And he
called his disciples to him, and said to them,
"Truly, I say to you, this poor widow has put in
more than all those who are contributing to the
treasury. For they all contributed out of their
abundance; but she out of her poverty has put
in everything she had, her whole living."
(Mark 12: 41-44)

Considerations

❖ What would Jesus say about the level of my generosity in supporting the Church and the various charities in need of assistance?

❖ To what extent am I motivated to give because of the recognition I would receive?

❖ How generous am I in giving my time when someone needs it?

❖ When is the last time I reevaluated the level of my giving based on my capacity to give? Am I being stingy?

❖ O God, you have given me so much in my life. Move me to be generous in giving back by helping others.

❖ Lord, help me to give until it hurts at least a little.

TREASURE THAT LASTS

And he told them a parable, saying, "The land of a rich man brought forth plentifully; and he thought to himself, 'What shall I do, for I have nowhere to store my crops?' And he said, 'I will do this: I will pull down my barns, and build larger ones; and there I will store all my grain and my goods. And I will say to my soul, Soul, you have ample goods laid up for many years; take your ease, eat, drink, be merry.' But God said to him, 'Fool! This night your soul is required of you; and the things you have prepared, whose will they be?' So is he who lays up treasure for himself, and is not rich toward God." (Luke 12: 16-21)

Considerations

❖ My life is out of balance if it is driven solely by material goals. What kind of priority do I place on receiving the sacraments regularly? Am I taking the time to pray and study the faith?

❖ Fostering a supernatural outlook will help me to avoid being unduly attached to the things of this world.

❖ Lord, help me to regard my material possessions as simply a means to serve you and society. Help me never to see them as ends in themselves.

❖ The treasure that I must seek is your grace, O Lord. Give me a thirst for the supernatural gifts you want to give me.

❖ Lord, may your warning of "Fool!" wake me up and move me to seek a life of holiness.

❖ Lord, help me to be generous with the material blessings you have given me.

Resisting Temptation and Sin

OCCASIONS OF SIN

"If your right eye causes you to sin, pluck it out and throw it away; it is better that you lose one of your members than that your whole body be thrown into hell." (Matthew 5: 29)

Considerations

❖ My occasions of sin could be a person, place, or thing that tends to lead me into sin.

❖ What are the occasions of sin that I need to avoid?

❖ Are there people whom I should avoid?

❖ Surfing the internet can be a problem. Can I restrict my internet use to those times when I have specific needs?

❖ I can bring up my occasions of sin in Confession. The priest can give me advice on how to avoid those situations.

❖ Lord, help me to see these occasions of sin clearly. Show me how to avoid them consistently.

❖ Being brutally honest with myself will help me to identify those situations that can lead me farther from you, Jesus.

❖ Lord, please give me the grace to face up to my weaknesses.

INTERIOR SINS

"You have heard that it was said to the men of old, 'You shall not kill; and whoever kills shall be liable to judgment.' But I say to you that every one who is angry with his brother shall be liable to judgment..." (Matthew 5: 21-22)

Considerations

❖ Have I committed interior sins? Do I have illicit thoughts? Desires? Do I indulge in envy? anger? lust?

❖ Have I been dismissive of the dangers of these sins simply because I did not act upon them?

❖ Making light of interior sins can be a sign of lukewarmness that may put my interior life in jeopardy.

❖ When temptations arise, I will quickly try to invoke Our Lord or Our Blessed Mother and ask for protection.

❖ A good examination of conscience can help me to identify my weaknesses and root out these tendencies.

❖ Lord, help me to avoid the occasions of interior sins.

❖ Jesus, move me to bring these sins to Confession. Confessing my interior sins in the Sacrament of Penance gives me the actual grace I need to avoid these sins in the future.

SUPERNATURAL OUTLOOK

"Come to me, all who labor and are heavy
laden, and I will give you rest. Take my yoke
upon you, and learn from me; for I am gentle
and lowly in heart, and you will find rest for
your souls. For my yoke is easy, and my
burden is light." (Matthew 11: 28-30)

Considerations

❖ "I can do all things in him who strengthens me." (Phil. 4: 13)

❖ Life can be a great struggle with hardships and sorrows. Jesus, these words give me comfort when I am tempted to feel sorry for myself.

❖ My defects and shortcomings can weigh me down sometimes. It is easy to get discouraged when I fail to make the progress I would like to make. Jesus, your invitation to rest in you gives me hope and reassurance.

❖ Lord Jesus, help me to hand my burden over to you. When I do so, it becomes your burden and is lighter and easier to bear.

❖ Jesus, taking your yoke upon me enables me to look beyond this world to the next. Looking to eternal life reminds me that life on earth is short, and life with you in heaven is endless.

❖ Lord, when I try to face the difficulties of life alone, I am prone to despair. Give me the grace to turn to you with confidence.

Uniting to the Church

THE POPE

"And I tell you, you are Peter, and on this rock I will build my church, and the powers of death shall not prevail against it. I will give you the keys of the kingdom of heaven, and whatever you bind on earth shall be bound in heaven, and whatever you loose on earth shall be loosed in heaven." (Matthew 16: 18-19)

When they had finished breakfast, Jesus said to Simon Peter, "Simon, son of John, do you love me more than these?" He said to him, "Yes, Lord; you know that I love you." He said to him, "Feed my lambs." (John 21: 15)

Considerations

❖ Saint Catherine of Siena called the pope "the sweet Christ on earth." He is the Vicar of Christ. Jesus has entrusted him to guide his Church in a very hostile world.

❖ Have I taken the time to read the documents that the pope has written? They were written for everyone's benefit, including mine. I will make a serious effort to stay abreast of the teachings of the Holy Father.

❖ The Holy Father needs our prayers and support. I will never let a day go by without praying for him.

❖ Lord, you made your Church hierarchical, with Peter as its head. Without a hierarchy and teaching authority, your Church could never have the unity that you so ardently prayed for at the Last Supper.

❖ Lord, give me a love for the pope, whomever he may be.

❖ Strengthen and protect the pope, dear Lord. You have given him a heavy burden to bear.

AUTHORITY OF THE CHURCH

"He who hears you hears me, and he who rejects you rejects me, and he who rejects me rejects him who sent me." (Luke 10: 16)

"But the Counselor, the Holy Spirit, whom the Father will send in my name, he will teach you all things, and bring to your remembrance all that I have said to you." (John 14: 26)

Considerations

❖ Am I really convinced that the Holy Spirit is guiding the Church?

❖ For more than 2,000 years, the Church has continued to shepherd its people— despite many crises, heresies, personal failings and sins of its hierarchy, and attacks from outside of the Church. Clearly, the Church is a Divine institution (as well as a human one), and God will protect her until the end of time.

❖ The Gospels make it clear that Jesus founded the Church and that he remains with us in the Church. He has not left us orphans.

❖ Jesus, make me, more and more, a child of the Church.

❖ Lord, help me to embrace wholeheartedly all the moral teachings of the Church because they are your teachings.

❖ My God, give me a deep love for the members of the hierarchy of the Church, despite their personal shortcomings.

Rejection of Christ

"He who rejects me and does not receive my
sayings has a judge; the word that I have
spoken will be his judge on the last day. For
I have not spoken on my own authority; the
Father who sent me has himself given me
commandment what to say and what to speak."
(John 12: 48-49)

Considerations

❖ Lord, I embrace all that you have taught us without reservation. Help me to be faithful to you all of my life.

❖ Jesus, your words are also spoken through your Church. I will look with confidence to Holy Mother Church for guidance and spiritual nourishment.

❖ Some of your moral teaching can be hard to accept. Help me to see that it is for my own good.

❖ Forgive me, Lord, for those times in my life when I wandered from you. Please do not allow me to ever stray from you and your Church again.

❖ When I sin, I reject you, my God, even when it is simply a matter of weakness. Lord, give me the strength to overcome temptation.

❖ Jesus, you were obedient to the Father and spoke all that he commanded you. I pray that you will meet me on the last day and say those words I long to hear, "Well done, good and faithful servant."
(Matthew 25: 23)

LIGHT OF FAITH

And Jesus cried out and said, "He who believes in me, believes not in me but in him who sent me. And he who sees me sees him who sent me. I have come as light into the world, that whoever believes in me may not remain in darkness." (John 12: 44-46)

Considerations

- ❖ Lord Jesus, you are always united to the Father. You are the window to the Father.

- ❖ Indeed, you are my path to unity with the Blessed Trinity.

- ❖ Jesus, your light shines on all people. Help me to be a lens through which your light shines on those whom I encounter each day.

- ❖ Whenever I turn from you, I am met with darkness.

- ❖ My Catholic faith provides a beacon of light that guides me throughout my life. Thank you, Lord, for the gift of faith!

- ❖ O God, increase my faith, hope, and love!

CHRISTIAN UNITY

"I do not pray for these only, but also for those
who believe in me through their word, that
they may all be one; even as thou, Father, art in
me, and I in thee, that they also may be in us,
so that the world may believe that thou hast
sent me. The glory which thou hast given me
I have given to them, that they may be one
even as we are one, I in them and thou in me,
that they may become perfectly one, so that the
world may know that thou hast sent me and
hast loved them even as thou hast loved me."
(John 17: 20-23)

Considerations

❖ Lord Jesus, you expressed your ardent desire for Christian unity at the Last Supper. Clearly, you desire a unity of faith within your otherwise diverse and universal Church.

❖ Lord, help me to foster that unity by reaching out to our separated brethren in love and understanding.

❖ You point to the Holy Trinity as the model for the unity you desire in your Church— three distinct Persons in one God. Lord, help me to see in your Church how we can be a diversity of cultures and rites while a unity in faith.

❖ Your hierarchy, with the pope at its head, ensures the unity that you desire. Give me a love for the pope and the bishops that transcends any human differences.

❖ As an apostle, I am called to promote Christian unity by sharing sound doctrine with my family and friends. Help me to stay abreast of the teachings of the Holy Father and my bishop so that I am better prepared to evangelize those around me.

❖ Lord Jesus, you have made it clear that you are counting on me to faithfully pass on the Gospel message to others. Give me the grace and courage to persevere in my apostolic endeavors.

Celebrating the Sacraments

MARRIAGE

And Pharisees came up and in order to test him asked, "Is it lawful for a man to divorce his wife?" He answered them, "What did Moses command you?" They said, "Moses allowed a man to write a certificate of divorce, and to put her away." But Jesus said to them, "For your hardness of heart he wrote you this commandment. But from the beginning of creation, 'God made them male and female.' 'For this reason a man shall leave his father and mother and be joined to his wife, and the two shall become one.' So they are no longer two but one. What therefore God has joined together, let not man put asunder."
(Mark 10: 2-9)

Considerations

- ❖ Marriage is a vocation from God, a lifelong commitment.

- ❖ We have become one flesh—an intimacy that embraces our entire relationship.

- ❖ My spouse is the most important person in my life. She/he is the object of my attitude of service at home.

- ❖ Dear Lord, help me to be a better husband/wife. Help me to be more attentive to her/his needs.

- ❖ Help me to make my home the school of love that you meant it to be.

- ❖ Show me where my selfishness has hurt our relationship and how I can make amends.

- ❖ Lord, thank you for giving her/him to me.

- ❖ True love is sacrificial. O God, help me to show my love with deeds.

MERCY OF GOD - HOPE

"Those who are well have no need of a physician, but those who are sick; I have not come to call the righteous, but sinners to repentance." (Luke 5: 31-32)

"Therefore I tell you, her sins, which are many, are forgiven, for she loved much; but he who is forgiven little, loves little." (Luke 7: 47)

"Jesus, remember me when you come in your kingly power." And he said to him, "Truly, I say to you, today you will be with me in Paradise." (Luke 23: 42-43)

Considerations

❖ How comforting, O Lord, to know that you
   have come to call sinners to repentance and
   that you are seeking me out, calling me
   to yourself.

❖ I am counting on your mercy, dear God.
   I beg you to overlook my many sins.

❖ In your mercy, you left us the Sacrament of
   Penance. Every time I approach the
   sacrament, I encounter you, Jesus. It is you
   to whom I confess. It is you who absolves
   me from my sins.

❖ Lord, teach me to love you like the woman
   who bathed your feet with her tears.
   May my love for you lead to a profound
   repentance and your forgiveness of my
   many sins.

❖ I am no better than the woman who was a
   sinner or the good thief who died with you
   on Calvary. Lord, help me to be as contrite
   as they were. May my sincere contrition
   move you to forgive me.

❖ I cannot fathom the depth of your mercy.
   There is no sin too grievous for you to
   forgive.

BORN AGAIN

Jesus answered, "Truly, truly, I say to you, unless one is born of water and the Spirit, he cannot enter the kingdom of God." (John 3: 5)

Considerations

❖ Jesus points to the necessity of Baptism for our salvation.

❖ I am also born again many times throughout my life.

❖ I was born again the day I made the Catholic faith my own.

❖ I am born again whenever I am restored to the state of grace in the Sacrament of Penance.

❖ I am born again every time I experience a conversion of heart and take a step closer to God.

❖ Through Baptism, I have "put on Christ" (Gal. 3: 27). Lord, help me to be faithful to all that this implies.

THE EUCHARIST

"He who eats my flesh and drinks my blood
has eternal life, and I will raise him up at the
last day. For my flesh is food indeed, and my
blood is drink indeed. He who eats my flesh
and drinks my blood abides in me, and I in
him." (John 6: 54-56)

Considerations

❖ The Church teaches that the Eucharist is "the source and summit of the Christian life." Does my Eucharistic piety reflect this truth?

❖ Why would I not want to witness the re-presentation of Christ's sacrifice on the Cross each day, if I could?

❖ Jesus, you feed me with your body, blood, soul, and divinity as often as I can worthily receive you. I cannot even begin to fathom the depths of your love for me.

❖ So often I am distracted during the celebration of the Mass. Forgive me, Lord, for being distracted. Help me to be better recollected. Help me to participate in the Mass more fervently.

❖ Lord, help me to be more generous in offering you the worship you desire.

❖ You wait for me in the tabernacle all day. Stopping by a church each day to say hello would be a small gesture of love.

CONFESSION

Jesus said to them again, "Peace be with you.
As the Father has sent me, even so I send you."
And when he had said this, he breathed on
them, and said to them, "Receive the Holy
Spirit. If you forgive the sins of any, they are
forgiven; if you retain the sins of any, they are
retained." (John 20: 21-23)

Considerations

❖ May I bring many souls to the sacrament of mercy.

❖ What a blessing we Catholics have to know with certainty that our sins are forgiven in the Sacrament of Confession. It is an incomparable source of peace.

❖ Remind me, Lord, that every time I confess my sins in the Sacrament of Penance, I encounter you.

❖ Jesus, in your wisdom, you knew that we needed this source of grace. And you knew the psychological benefit of confessing to another person who is empowered to forgive in your name.

❖ Lord, may I seek you out in the Sacrament of Penance without delay whenever I fall from grace. Let me feel that separation from you deep within my soul!

❖ Dear God, may my desire for holiness move me to frequent reception of the Sacrament of Confession. I need not bring only mortal sins to my encounter with you in the sacrament. I wish to bring you all of my failings, large and small.

Loving Jesus Christ

SPIRITUAL CHILDHOOD

And calling to him a child, he put him in the
midst of them, and said, "Truly, I say to you,
unless you turn and become like children, you
will never enter the kingdom of heaven.
Whoever humbles himself like this child, he is
the greatest in the kingdom of heaven."
(Matthew 18: 2-4)

Considerations

❖ Jesus makes it clear that I must have a childlike relationship with God, my Father.

❖ Having a childlike faith does not preclude my having a theologian's knowledge and understanding of the faith.

❖ My pride always leads me away from God who is my Father.

❖ Lord, give me the humility of a child.

❖ A child is completely dependent on his or her parents and trusting of them. O God, may my dependence on you deepen and foster a trust that cannot be shaken.

❖ Abba, Father, I rely on you for everything. You have given me so much! Please never cease blessing me. I need your continued blessings.

❖ Lord, help me to find any evidence of pride in my examination of conscience so that I can root it out.

GENEROSITY OF GOD

Jesus said, "Truly, I say to you, there is no one who has left house or brothers or sisters or mother or father or children or lands, for my sake and for the gospel, who will not receive a hundredfold now in this time, houses and brothers and sisters and mothers and children and lands, with persecutions, and in the age to come eternal life. But many that are first will be last, and the last first." (Mark 10: 29-31)

Considerations

❖ Heaven is an eternity in your presence, filled with indescribable joy in communion with the saints and my loved ones. What would I give to possess this?

❖ "What no eye has seen, nor ear heard, nor the heart of man conceived, what God has prepared for those who love him." (1 Cor. 2: 9)

❖ Lord, you offer me so much in exchange for my love!

❖ You offer me your friendship and eternal bliss—that is ETERNAL bliss, forever, without end—in exchange for a few short years of love and sacrifice and fidelity.

❖ Jesus, your friendship in this life gives me peace and comfort, despite any hardships that I may encounter.

❖ Lord, you offer me everything in exchange for a pittance.

SPIRIT OF SERVICE

But Jesus called them to him and said, "You know that the rulers of the Gentiles lord it over them, and their great men exercise authority over them. It shall not be so among you; but whoever would be great among you must be your servant, and whoever would be first among you must be your slave; even as the Son of man came not to be served but to serve, and to give his life as a ransom for many." (Matthew 20: 25-28)

When he had washed their feet, and taken his garments, and resumed his place, he said to them, "Do you know what I have done to you? You call me Teacher and Lord; and you are right, for so I am. If I then, your Lord and Teacher, have washed your feet, you also ought to wash one another's feet. For I have given you an example, that you also should do as I have done to you." (John 13: 12-15)

Considerations

❖ The Creator of the Universe washed the feet of his friends and followers. How can I be reluctant to serve my fellow man?

❖ One's greatness is measured by his or her willingness to serve the others.

❖ A saint puts the needs of brothers and sisters first.

❖ Caring for others may be a mortification— a sweet mortification that co-redeems.

❖ To be the servant of others is to be Christ-like.

❖ Lord, forgive me for being so wrapped up in my own concerns. Give me the generosity of spirit to reach out to those in need.

THE NEED FOR REPENTANCE

"What do you think? A man had two sons; and he went to the first and said, 'Son, go and work in the vineyard today.' And he answered, 'I will not'; but afterward he repented and went. And he went to the second and said the same; and he answered, 'I go, sir,' but did not go. Which of the two did the will of his father?" They said, "The first." Jesus said to them, "Truly, I say to you, the tax collectors and the harlots go into the kingdom of God before you." (Matthew 21: 28-31)

Considerations

❖ My sorrow should be reflected in the way I live my life—sacrifice, atonement, and reparation, all done cheerfully.

❖ Lord, help me to cultivate a sincere spirit of repentance. My sins warrant a lifetime of atonement.

❖ Lord, how can I make up to you for all of my infidelities?

❖ I must remember that my repentance should be reflected in my deeds, not only in my words.

❖ My God, when I consider all that you have done for me and how I continue to turn my back on you, I can only weep with a sorrow born of love. May my tears give rise to a firm resolution to change so that I can become the apostle you called me to be.

❖ Lord, please give me the grace to use my time well, devoting my life to your service. A life of service is a small price to pay in reparation for my offenses against my Savior.

CHRISTIAN LOVE

Jesus answered, "The first is, 'Hear, O Israel:
The Lord our God, the Lord is one; and you
shall love the Lord your God with all your
heart, and with all your soul, and with all your
mind, and with all your strength.' The second
is this, 'You shall love your neighbor as
yourself.' There is no other commandment
greater than these." (Mark 12: 29-31)

"A new commandment I give to you, that you
love one another; even as I have loved you,
that you also love one another. By this all men
will know that you are my disciples, if you
have love for one another." (John 13: 34-35)

Considerations

- ❖ Loving God is not a part-time affair. God asks us to love him with all of our being.

- ❖ What is there in my life that I am placing ahead of God? What is preventing me from loving him as he wishes?

- ❖ "Love is patient and kind; love is not jealous or boastful; it is not arrogant or rude. Love does not insist on its own way; it is not irritable or resentful; it does not rejoice at wrong, but rejoices in the right. Love bears all things, believes all things, hopes all things, endures all things." (1 Cor. 13: 4-7)

- ❖ Lord, your call to love you with all of my being is a call to holiness. I know that I have a long way to go on the path to holiness. But, with your grace, I can achieve it. You would not ask me to do something that I cannot do.

- ❖ Jesus, you have asked me to love my neighbor as you have loved me with a sacrificial love.

- ❖ Lord, help me to consider the needs of others first.

ADORATION OF GOD

Now when Jesus was at Bethany in the house of Simon the leper, a woman came up to him with an alabaster jar of very expensive ointment, and she poured it on his head, as he sat at table. But when the disciples saw it, they were indignant, saying, "Why this waste? For this ointment might have been sold for a large sum, and given to the poor." But Jesus, aware of this, said to them, "Why do you trouble the woman? For she has done a beautiful thing to me. For you always have the poor with you, but you will not always have me. In pouring this ointment on my body she has done it to prepare me for burial. Truly, I say to you, wherever this gospel is preached in the whole world, what she has done will be told in memory of her." (Matthew 26: 6-13)

Considerations

❖ When do I choose to spend time with you in prayer—those leftover hours when I am tired and distracted or those hours when I am most alert?

❖ How do I dress for Sunday Mass? If I could go from Mass to a picnic without changing, my dress probably does not reflect the importance of that time of Divine worship.

❖ Distractions during Mass happen. I am human. But, do I struggle enough to avoid them?

❖ Dear Lord, nothing is too good for offering you my praise and adoration.

❖ A chalice made of gold and precious gems, vestments of the highest quality, stained glass, and inspiring art, incense and bells, angels singing. None of this even begins to be worthy of your majesty, O Lord.

❖ Jesus, I promise to give you my best—in my prayer and in my work.

❖ Lord, help me to be generous in offering you the best I have to offer.

PRESENCE OF CHRIST

"Go therefore and make disciples of all
nations, baptizing them in the name of the
Father and of the Son and of the Holy Spirit,
teaching them to observe all that I have
commanded you; and lo, I am with you always,
to the close of the age." (Matthew 28: 19-20)

Considerations

- ❖ How often I act as if Jesus is nowhere around me, as if he has no idea what I am doing or thinking.

- ❖ I must remember that it is not I who brings souls closer to you. It is the Holy Spirit. I am only an instrument.

- ❖ Jesus, forgive me for ignoring you so often throughout the day.

- ❖ Lord, you choose to stay close to me, to offer me comfort and friendship. Help me to embrace that friendship. I will try harder to nurture our friendship with conversation and sacrifice.

- ❖ As your disciple, you have asked me to share my faith with others, to share the good news. In doing so, I know that I may rely on your grace. You are by my side always.

- ❖ Even when things appear to be going badly, you are with me. I know you will never abandon me.

IMPORTANCE OF GOOD EXAMPLE

"Whoever causes one of these little ones who believe in me to sin, it would be better for him if a great millstone were hung round his neck and he were thrown into the sea." (Mark 9: 42)

Considerations

❖ My example can influence so many people—for good or for bad.

❖ We cannot know in this life the total repercussions of our actions. We could set up a chain reaction that goes on for generations.

❖ The general judgment will reveal to all the extent of the good that I have done and the extent of the evil.

❖ Lord, forgive me for the many times that I have given bad example.

❖ As a Christian, I am called to a higher standard. Lord, help me to live up to my calling.

❖ Lord, you make it clear that it will not go well for those who lead others to sin. Please give me time to atone for all the damage I have done.

THE NATIVITY

And Joseph also went up from Galilee, from
the city of Nazareth, to Judea, to the city of
David, which is called Bethlehem, because he
was of the house and lineage of David, to be
enrolled with Mary, his betrothed, who was
with child. And while they were there, the time
came for her to be delivered. And she gave
birth to her first-born son and wrapped him in
swaddling cloths, and laid him in a manger,
because there was no place for them in the inn.
(Luke 2: 4-7)

Considerations

❖ Contemplate the pure love of Mary and Joseph. Joseph cherishes Mary as his wife and his love, and Mary's heart swells as she watches Joseph tenderly care for her child.

❖ My God, what humility you show by becoming a mere man! You lowered yourself to such a degree. How could I ever question your love for humanity? How could I ever question your love for me?

❖ Lord, you could have come into the world in comfortable surroundings. Instead, you chose poverty to teach us that love is the wellspring of family life and that material possessions have little importance.

❖ O God, you chose to become the most vulnerable of creatures, totally dependent on Mary and Joseph for protection and sustenance.

❖ It is instructive that only the humble are witnesses to this blessed event—heavenly angels, poor shepherds, and wise men who sought to worship the infant king. Jesus, help me to grow in humility so that I too can embrace you and rock you in my arms.

HUMANITY OF CHRIST

When Jesus saw her weeping, and the Jews who came with her also weeping, he was deeply moved in spirit and troubled; and he said, "Where have you laid him?" They said to him, "Lord, come and see." Jesus wept. (John 11: 33-35)

And he said to them, "My soul is very sorrowful, even to death; remain here, and watch." And going a little farther, he fell on the ground and prayed that, if it were possible, the hour might pass from him. And he said, "Abba, Father, all things are possible to thee; remove this cup from me; yet not what I will, but what thou wilt." (Mark 14: 34-36)

Considerations

❖ God is love, said Saint John (1 John 4:8). What better proof is there than God's willingness to share our limitations and to take on our human nature to teach us how to love?

❖ Jesus, while on earth, you were a man with emotions and weaknesses, like me.

❖ You were hungry and thirsty. You laughed and cried. You knew joy and pain.

❖ Jesus, I know that you love me with the same human heart with which you loved Lazarus and your other disciples. Never let me forget your love for me!

❖ Lord, your human nature could hardly bear the prospect of your Passion. Yet, out of love, you united your human will to the Divine will and suffered an excruciating death for the forgiveness of sins.

❖ My God, give me the grace to unite my will to yours. Let my constant prayer be, "Thy will be done on earth as it is in heaven."

OBLIGATIONS OF THOSE BLESSED BY GOD

"… Every one to whom much is given, of him will much be required; and of him to whom men commit much they will demand the more." (Luke 12: 48)

Considerations

❖ If not for God's mercy, this teaching would worry me greatly! I have been given so much.

❖ My faith, my family, my health, my freedom, my friends, my material possessions—a life is too short for giving back all that is required of me.

❖ A lifetime of plenty must be answered with a spirit of sacrifice and a life of holiness.

❖ For a Christian, one's self-giving can never be enough.

❖ Lord, help me to see your will for me. Please give me a generous heart. Show me how to channel my generosity according to your will.

❖ Jesus, I know you are asking more of me. Show me where I have been holding back.

FREEDOM

Jesus then said to the Jews who had believed in
him, "If you continue in my word, you are
truly my disciples, and you will know the truth,
and the truth will make you free."
(John 8: 31-32)

Jesus answered them, "Truly, truly, I say to
you, every one who commits sin is a slave to
sin." (John 8: 34)

Considerations

- ❖ The moral law has been given to me so that I may flourish, so that I may be happy.

- ❖ My sins weigh me down. They make me sluggish as I focus on myself, as I turn inward.

- ❖ I am most free when I live according to your will, O Lord!

- ❖ I was created for you, my God. When you are my reference point, I soar like an eagle.

- ❖ Am I attached to any sins, even venial sins? Lord, help me to break free of these attachments. I wish to be free of my enslavement!

- ❖ Am I availing myself of the Sacrament of Penance on a regular basis? Lord, I know you are calling me to this sacrament of mercy. This encounter with you is what I need to be strengthened to break free of the shackles of sin.

SANCTIFYING GRACE

Jesus said to her, "I am the resurrection and the life; he who believes in me, though he die, yet shall he live, and whoever lives and believes in me shall never die." (John 11: 25-26)

Considerations

❖ Lord Jesus, you promise me eternal life if I believe in you and conform my life to yours.

❖ The life you offer me is not the mortal life that will end when I breathe my last breath. It is the supernatural life, the life of grace that will enable me to behold your face in heaven for all eternity.

❖ Lord, without the sacraments, I would be like the walking dead, full of smiles and bodily warmth on the outside but a rotting corpse on the inside.

❖ I too cry out to you with tears, Lord: "I believe; help my unbelief!" (Mark 9: 24)

❖ Lord, never let me stray from your side. It is life that I want, life forever in your presence.

❖ Jesus, help me to grow in grace. You have called me to a life of sanctity, a life of holiness that could be a model for others.

THE WAY

Jesus said to him, "I am the way, and the truth, and the life; no one comes to the Father, but by me." (John 14: 6)

Considerations

- ❖ Jesus, how could I fail to make you the center of my life?

- ❖ Lord, you offer me everything I need to have happiness, especially eternal happiness.

- ❖ You are the way. Following you means a life of love, sacrifice, pursuit of the virtues, unity with the Father...

- ❖ You are the truth. Your life and teaching provide me with what I need to reach eternal life, if I strive to embrace them. As true God and true man, you are Truth personified.

- ❖ You are the life. Lord, you nourish me with your body, blood, soul, and divinity— without which I have no life within me.

- ❖ Lord, as I reflect on your words, I ask you to move me to make a firm resolution to follow the way to which you have called me, to read and meditate on the truth of the Gospels, and to partake frequently in the Bread of Life at your Eucharistic Banquet.

OUR DEPENDENCY ON CHRIST

"I am the true vine, and my Father is the
vinedresser. Every branch of mine that bears
no fruit, he takes away, and every branch that
does bear fruit he prunes, that it may bear more
fruit. You are already made clean by the word
which I have spoken to you. Abide in me, and
I in you. As the branch cannot bear fruit by
itself, unless it abides in the vine, neither can
you, unless you abide in me. I am the vine, you
are the branches. He who abides in me, and I in
him, he it is that bears much fruit, for apart
from me you can do nothing." (John 15: 1-5)

Considerations

- ❖ Without you, Lord, I can do nothing! This is a fact that, unfortunately, I have had to learn the hard way.

- ❖ Lord, help me to see the hardships that I face as the pruning that I must endure to be fruitful and to be closer to you.

- ❖ Any success that I have in the apostolate is due solely to your action. I am merely an instrument. Separated from you, I am as useful as the dead branch that falls to the ground.

- ❖ Just as you are the vine, Lord, so is your Church. Keep me firmly attached to your Church as she is the source of my sustenance.

- ❖ Jesus, help me to unite myself more closely to you. Reading the Gospels, receiving the Eucharist and the Sacrament of Penance, and engaging in mental prayer are sure ways to unity with you.

- ❖ Jesus, you ask me to abide in you! How can I do otherwise, my Friend, my Savior?

FRIENDSHIP OF CHRIST

"Greater love has no man than this, that a man lay down his life for his friends. You are my friends if you do what I command you. No longer do I call you servants, for the servant does not know what his master is doing; but I have called you friends, for all that I have heard from my Father I have made known to you." (John 15: 13-15)

Considerations

❖ Jesus, may I never take for granted the friendship you have offered me.

❖ Lord, you taught me how to be a good friend. You made yourself vulnerable and shared with me what is most dear to you.

❖ Jesus, you suffered an agonizing death for me—for me! You would have suffered your Passion and Death for me alone!

❖ Surely, obedience to your commands is not too much to ask of a friend who owes you everything.

❖ How much am I willing to give up for you? An hour a day? Several hours a week? A lifetime? For our friendship to thrive, I need to give of myself. I need to invest in our friendship.

❖ Help me to grasp the reality that you, the Creator of the Universe, have sought me out for my friendship.

THE RESURRECTION

But on the first day of the week, at early dawn, they went to the tomb, taking the spices which they had prepared. And they found the stone rolled away from the tomb, but when they went in they did not find the body. While they were perplexed about this, behold, two men stood by them in dazzling apparel; and as they were frightened and bowed their faces to the ground, the men said to them, "Why do you seek the living among the dead? He is not here, but has risen. Remember how he told you, while he was still in Galilee, that the Son of man must be delivered into the hands of sinful men, and be crucified, and on the third day rise."
(Luke 24: 1-7)

Considerations

❖ Jesus, you are alive and with us. Your victory over death fills us with joy.

❖ Lord, your Resurrection is the pivotal event of history. If you had not risen as you said you would, we would have no basis for our faith. As Saint Paul said, "If Christ has not been raised, then our preaching is in vain and your faith is in vain." (1 Cor. 15: 14)

❖ Jesus, after the Resurrection you continued to instruct your disciples and reassure them. What love and patience you showed to Peter who denied you three times, to Thomas who would not believe without touching your wounds himself, and to the disciples on the road to Emmaus who did not believe that you had risen.

❖ Jesus, your Resurrection confirms your divinity to all the world. You are true man and true God. That my Creator would go to such lengths to draw me to himself for all eternity is a mystery indeed—a mystery of Love!

❖ I can imagine the great joy that filled the Apostles and other disciples. You appeared to hundreds of your disciples—encouraging them and instilling in them an apostolic zeal that, through the Holy Spirit, helped your Church expand to the ends of the earth. Lord, give me an apostolic zeal that will never fade.

Honoring Mary, Mother of God

THE GREATNESS OF MARY

And he came to her and said, "Hail, full of grace, the Lord is with you!" (Luke 1: 28)

"Blessed are you among women, and blessed is the fruit of your womb! And why is this granted me, that the mother of my Lord should come to me?" (Luke 1: 42-43)

And Mary said, "My soul magnifies the Lord, and my spirit rejoices in God my Savior, for he has regarded the low estate of his handmaiden. For behold, henceforth all generations will call me blessed; for he who is mighty has done great things for me, and holy is his name." (Luke 1: 46-49)

Considerations

❖ The Holy Rosary is my weapon of choice in my spiritual struggle. I pray the Rosary every day for all of my intentions.

❖ Mary, you are the masterpiece of God's grace! No one embraced the will of God more faithfully than you.

❖ God preserved you from any stain of sin. He chose you to bear his son and become the mother of all humanity.

❖ Mary, my mother, protect me from all temptations. Keep me safe from the snares set before me. I run to you to immediately banish from my mind any thoughts that are impure or unbecoming of a child of God.

❖ You are the greatest of God's creatures and the humblest. Teach me to approach you and the Lord as a little child approaches his or her mother and father.

❖ Mary, I run to you in time of need, knowing that you will not deny your little child any good thing that I ask for with faith and humility.

MARY'S ADVICE

On the third day there was a marriage at Cana in Galilee, and the mother of Jesus was there; Jesus also was invited to the marriage, with his disciples. When the wine failed, the mother of Jesus said to him, "They have no wine." And Jesus said to her, "O woman, what have you to do with me? My hour has not yet come." His mother said to the servants, "Do whatever he tells you." (John 2: 1-5)

Considerations

❖ Mary is such a powerful intercessor. She prevailed upon Jesus at Cana to save their friends from embarrassment. I will go to you, dear Mary, in my time of need.

❖ Mary instructs the attendants to do whatever Jesus tells them. Could there be any better advice? Mary, help me to follow the commandments of your son throughout my life.

❖ Your friendship brought the family at Cana closer to Jesus. Help me to bring my friends closer to the Lord through my words and example.

❖ By following the instructions of Jesus, the attendants facilitated a great miracle. Mary, help me to be an effective instrument in God's hands. My docility to God's grace and promptings can lead to great things. With the grace of God, I can re-evangelize my little corner of the world.

❖ Mary, you did not have to attend the wedding at Cana. But your friendship and love for your friends moved you to attend and elevate the spiritual temperature of the affair. Your presence changed everything. I, too, can venture out among my friends and others, and, with my Christian demeanor, raise the spiritual temperature of those around me.

MARY, OUR MOTHER

When Jesus saw his mother, and the disciple whom he loved standing near, he said to his mother, "Woman, behold, your son!" Then he said to the disciple, "Behold, your mother!" And from that hour the disciple took her to his own home. (John 19: 26-27)

Considerations

❖ As Jesus was dying on the cross, he entrusted his mother, Mary, to John, and he gave John to Mary. John represents all mankind. Jesus knew what we need to be his disciples. We need his mother to protect and guide us.

❖ When I pray the Rosary, I seek to meditate on the mysteries of that day. As I focus on the mysteries, I recite the Hail Marys as sweet background music.

❖ Mary, stay by my side always. Never leave me!

❖ I look with affection at your image on the wall in my home. You are my mother, and I am your child.

❖ I try to foster my closeness to you through prayer and the many Marian devotions the Church recommends.

❖ Mother, forgive me for offending your son, my brother, so often. With your help, I can be reconciled to him as I seek his forgiveness in the Sacrament of Confession.

Accepting Suffering

THE CROSS

Then Jesus told his disciples, "If any man would come after me, let him deny himself and take up his cross and follow me. For whoever would save his life will lose it, and whoever loses his life for my sake will find it. For what will it profit a man, if he gains the whole world and forfeits his life? Or what shall a man give in return for his life? (Matthew 16: 24-26)

Considerations

- ❖ I know that offering small acts of self-denial will bring me closer to God.

- ❖ By voluntarily bearing the small crosses of each day, I prepare myself to take up the big crosses that will come my way.

- ❖ Lord, you have made it clear that the cross is an essential part of the Christian vocation. Yet, so many times I find myself avoiding the cross—even little crosses that I could easily bear.

- ❖ My love of comfort is an obstacle to my growth in holiness. Lord, help me to embrace the cross in the little things of each day.

- ❖ Help me to unite my crosses to your cross, dear Lord.

- ❖ I will seek a little cold, heat, discomfort, hunger, or thirst, and I will unite these discomforts to your Passion, O Lord. How valuable they become as they co-redeem along with you.

MORTIFICATION

"Truly, truly, I say to you, unless a grain of
wheat falls into the earth and dies, it remains
alone; but if it dies, it bears much fruit. He who
loves his life loses it, and he who hates his life
in this world will keep it for eternal life."
(John 12: 24-25)

Considerations

❖ How can I expect to handle the big challenges in life—those that may be faith-shaking—if I cannot offer to God a little voluntary discomfort when things are going well?

❖ My voluntary acts of self-denial train my will, help me to focus less on myself, and be more like Christ, the suffering servant.

❖ Is self-denial a part of my spiritual life? Am I willing to suffer, even a little, for the one who gave his life for me?

❖ Dear Lord, give me a spirit of sacrifice that will bear much fruit.

❖ There is no love without sacrifice. My willingness to deny myself is an expression of my love for you, my Lord.

❖ A person in love will do anything for the beloved—sacrifice comfort, give gifts, and go out of the way to please the beloved. What do I do for you, my God, to show you how much I love you?

❖ Lord, help me to discern what small mortifications I can offer you each day, mortifications that no one else will notice.

CHRIST'S PASSION AND DEATH

And when they came to the place which is
called The Skull, there they crucified him, and
the criminals, one on the right and one on the
left. And Jesus said, "Father, forgive them; for
they know not what they do." And they cast
lots to divide his garments. (Luke 23: 33-34)

It was now about the sixth hour, and there was
darkness over the whole land until the ninth
hour, while the sun's light failed; and the
curtain of the temple was torn in two. Then
Jesus, crying with a loud voice, said, "Father,
into thy hands I commit my spirit!" And
having said this he breathed his last.
(Luke 23: 44-46)

Considerations

❖ Jesus, you did not have to suffer all that you did to redeem us. A single drop of your precious blood would have been sufficient. Yet, you wanted to give everything for the love of your people, for the love of me.

❖ My sins put you on the cross. Each of my sins led to the mocking, the scourging, and the hammer blows driving the nails through your hands and feet. Forgive me, Jesus, and give me the grace of repentance. Lord, help me to resolve never to offend you again.

❖ As you hung from the cross gasping for breath, your entire being was immersed in love. Help me to see your act of redemption as something very personal. Yes, you redeemed all mankind. But, you, my God, were also looking into my eyes, into my soul, forgiving me.

❖ Lord, your Passion and Death are re-presented to me in an unbloody manner at every Mass. May my sorrow be renewed at each Mass I attend—accompanied by a firm resolution to change.

❖ The horror of your Passion and Death makes clear to all the undeniable ugliness of sin.

❖ Lord, you suffered all of this for me. What am I willing to do for you?

Preparing to Meet God

READY FOR DEATH

"Afterward the other maidens came also, saying, 'Lord, lord, open to us.' But he replied, 'Truly, I say to you, I do not know you.' Watch therefore, for you know neither the day nor the hour." (Matthew 25: 11-13)

'And I will say to my soul, Soul, you have ample goods laid up for many years; take your ease, eat, drink, be merry.' But God said to him, 'Fool! This night your soul is required of you; and the things you have prepared, whose will they be?' (Luke 12: 19-20)

Considerations

❖ Am I overly concerned with the material things in life? Can I put more trust in Divine Providence? Focusing on worldly matters at the expense of those of eternal significance may lead me to receive that chastisement from God: "Fool!"

❖ Am I ready to die tonight in my sleep?

❖ What a terrifying thought that when all is said and done, Our Lord greets me with the words, "I do not know you!" Lord, spare me that fate. Help me to love you with all my heart.

❖ Jesus, I want to be the friend whom you will embrace warmly when I meet you at the end of my life.

❖ Too often I could be rightly accused of being most interested in relaxing, eating, drinking, and being merry. Dear God, give me time to atone for my thoughtless and easygoing life.

❖ Lord, may I always be prepared for my definitive encounter with you. Frequent Confessions, examinations of conscience, mortifications, devotions to Our Lady, and daily conversations with you will make my passage to the next life a continuum of love to Love.

PROMISE OF SALVATION

"Let not your hearts be troubled; believe in
God, believe also in me. In my Father's house
are many rooms; if it were not so, would I have
told you that I go to prepare a place for you?
And when I go and prepare a place for you,
I will come again and will take you to myself,
that where I am you may be also. And you
know the way where I am going."
(John 14: 1-4)

Considerations

❖ Jesus, these tender words to your disciples are words of love and understanding.

❖ Lord, help me to see the simple truth that these words of hope were also addressed to me personally.

❖ My Lord, you are my destiny! I was created to be with you forever in heaven.

❖ My focus must be on the life to come. Lord, every aspect of my life should be seasoned with the knowledge of your love and the place you have prepared for me in heaven.

❖ Jesus, you want me to be with you forever in Paradise. I pray that I will be ready on the day you come to take me to yourself.

❖ Lord, the words of Saint Paul fill me with hope and expectation, "What no eye has seen, nor ear heard, nor the heart of man conceived, what God has prepared for those who love him," (1 Cor. 2: 9)

HEAVEN

"And this is eternal life, that they know thee the only true God, and Jesus Christ whom thou hast sent." (John 17: 3)

Considerations

❖ Saint Paul tells us that heaven will be more wonderful than we can possibly imagine.

❖ An eternity of ineffable love spent with God, the Blessed Mother, the saints, and my loved ones. Now that is a party that I do not want to miss!

❖ Heaven must be beyond wonderful because its entry price is the blood of God himself.

❖ Union with you for all eternity, that is what I strive for, with your grace and the means offered to me by your Church.

❖ Heaven must begin here on earth as I grow closer to you, O God, and come to know you more through prayer and study.

❖ A very holy priest I knew (may he rest in peace) used to say that many of us want to go to heaven only in view of the alternative. I think he was only partly joking. Lord, motivated by love, may I long to be with you simply because I long to be with you.

ACCOUNTABILITY

"I tell you, on the day of judgment men will render account for every careless word they utter; for by your words you will be justified, and by your words you will be condemned." (Matthew 12: 36-37)

Considerations

❖ My judgment is coming! May it be a joyful encounter with my Savior as he says, 'Well done, good and faithful servant … enter into the joy of your master.' (Matthew 25: 23).

❖ I have so much for which to atone!

❖ I will be judged for so much more than my careless words. I have offended you, Jesus, in so many ways—sins of commission and sins of omission.

❖ The thought of my judgment would be truly terrifying if not for my confidence in your mercy and love.

❖ Lord, give me a contrite heart and the time to atone for my many sins.

❖ My God, in your mercy you have given me the opportunity to accuse myself in the Sacrament of Confession of sinning against you. Lord, move me to take advantage of this sacrament of mercy frequently.

HELL

"Just as the weeds are gathered and burned with fire, so will it be at the close of the age. The Son of man will send his angels, and they will gather out of his kingdom all causes of sin and all evildoers, and throw them into the furnace of fire; there men will weep and gnash their teeth. Then the righteous will shine like the sun in the kingdom of their Father. He who has ears, let him hear." (Matthew 13: 40-43)

Considerations

❖ Hell is a reality!

❖ God will not send me to hell. If I go there, it is because I choose to go there. My choice is expressed by the way I live my life.

❖ When I sin gravely, I turn away from God. I effectively put God out of my life. If I die without repenting of my mortal sins, I will have rejected God definitively, choosing to spend eternity without him.

❖ Hell is separation from God for all eternity. We were created for union with him, and the pain of separation from God is beyond description. In hell, we deny ourselves the Divine union for which we were made.

❖ Scripture describes hell as a "furnace of fire," suggesting an eternity of physical suffering compounded by the spiritual and emotional pain of loss.

❖ Lord, give me a profound hatred of sin—both venial and mortal. I must remember that my lukewarmness, my willingness to commit deliberate venial sins, disposes me to commit mortal sins. It puts me at hell's doorstep!

❖ My Lord, I never want to be separated from you.

About the Author

Stephen Gabriel was born in Quincy, Massachusetts. The son of a merchant sea captain and a homemaker, he moved with his parents and five siblings to Fort Lauderdale, Florida, and then to the Panama Canal Zone, where he attended high school.

He graduated from Loyola University of Chicago with a B.A. in economics. He received an M.S. in finance and a Ph.D. in agricultural economics from the University of Illinois.

Gabriel and his wife, Peggy, have been married 46 years. They have eight adult children and 35 grandchildren. He is a retired agricultural economist with the federal government.

Gabriel is the author of three books on fatherhood, *To Be A Father: 200 Promises that Will Transform You, Your Marriage and Your Family*, *Speaking to the Heart: A Father's Guide to Growth in Virtue* and *The Indispensable Dad: A Guide to Cultivating*

Family Happiness, Virtue and Success.
He is the editor of *Catholic Controversies:
Understanding Church Teaching and Events
in History*. He recently wrote a book for
grandparents entitled *Hope for you
Grandchildren: Talking to the Third
Generation About What Matters.*

Alone with Jesus: Praying with the Gospels,
his most recent book, is the product of many
years of struggling to pray well. The struggle
continues as he tries to take small steps closer
to Our Lord while conversing with him and
listening to his words in the Gospels.

Made in the USA
Middletown, DE
05 April 2023

28297774R00084